Educators Love STEP-U~~
So Do Children

In this exciting series:

• THE WORDS ARE HARDER (but not too hard)

• THERE'S A LOT MORE TEXT (but it's in bigger print)

• THERE ARE PLENTY OF ILLUSTRATIONS (but they are not just picture books)

• And the subject matter has been carefully chosen to appeal to young readers who want to find out about the world for themselves. These informative and lively books are just the answer.

*"STEP-UP BOOKS

. . . fill a need for precise informational material written in a simple readable form which children can and will enjoy. More please!"—EVELYN L. HEADLEY, *Director of Elementary Education, Edison, New Jersey.*

"I love them."—STEVE MEYER, *second grade pupil, Chicago, Illinois.*

FISH DO THE STRANGEST THINGS Fish that fish, fish that fly, even fish that climb trees! These are just a few of the astonishing fishes to be found in this book. It will prove to the young reader that fascinating facts can be as much fun as fiction.

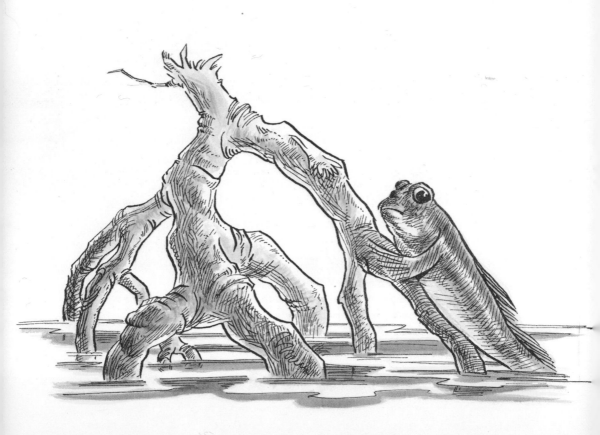

FISH
do the
STRANGEST
THINGS

By Leonora and Arthur Hornblow

Illustrations by Michael K. Frith

Step-Up Books · Random House

New York

FOR CALLEY AND CHRISTINA

LEONORA & ARTHUR HORNBLOW are the co-authors of four books in the unique Step-Up nature series: *Animals Do the Strangest Things, Birds Do the Strangest Things, Fish Do the Strangest Things,* and *Insects Do the Strangest Things.*

Arthur Hornblow, Jr. is best known as the movie producer who made such famous films as *Oklahoma, Weekend at the Waldorf, Gaslight* and *Witness for the Prosecution.*

Leonora Hornblow is a columnist, novelist, and author of historical books for children.

The Hornblows live in New York City where they are Associate Members of the American Museum of Natural History and the New York Zoological Society.

MICHAEL K. FRITH is from Bermuda and is a Harvard graduate. At Harvard he co-authored the acclaimed parody thriller *Alligator,* majored in Fine Arts, and was president of the *Harvard Lampoon.* He has since illustrated all four of the Hornblows' books and several books for adults.

Mr. Frith, his wife and two daughters live in New York, where he works as an illustrator, designer and editor of children's books.

This title was originally catalogued by the Library of Congress as follows: Hornblow, Leonora. Fish do the strangest things, by Leonora and Arthur Hornblow. Illus. by Michael K. Frith. New York, Random House [1966] 60 p. col. illus. 22 cm. (Step-up books) 1. Fishes—Juvenile literature. I. Hornblow, Arthur, joint author. II. Frith, Michael K., illus. III. Title. PZ10.H78Fi j 597 66-15486 ISBN 0-394-80062-1   ISBN 0-394-90062-6 (lib. bdg.)

Contents

FISH DO THE STRANGEST THINGS

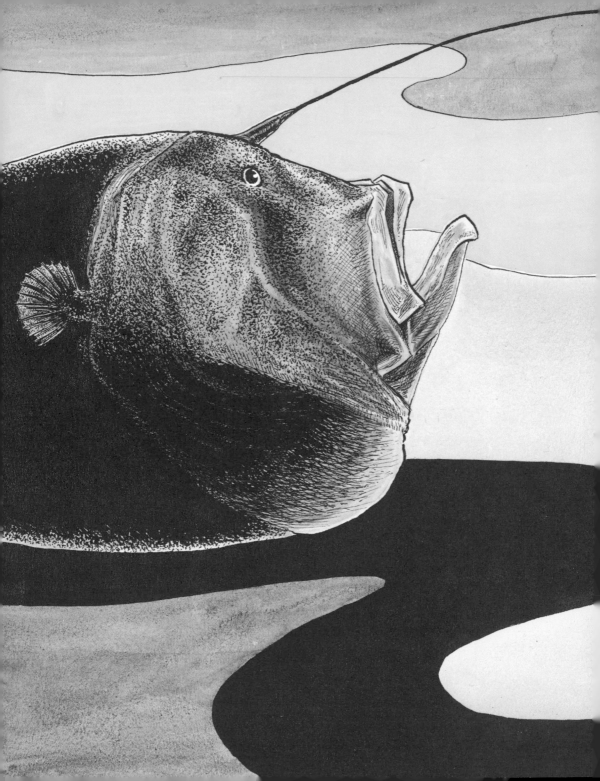

The Fish
That Goes Fishing

Fishermen catch many strange fish. But one of the strangest fish of all does her own fishing. She lives down deep in the dark sea. She is called the deep-sea angler.

The deep-sea angler has her own fishing rod. It grows out of the top of her head and hangs in front of her mouth. The tip of her rod shines in the deep dark water. This tip is the bait on her fishing rod.

3

Hungry fish see her bait. They think it is something to eat. A hungry fish will swim toward the shiny bait. The angler opens her wide mouth. The fish swims closer and closer. He swims right at the bait. Then the angler closes her mouth. Snap! That's the end of that fish.

The female deep-sea angler may grow to be three feet long. But her husband is very much smaller. He is only about three inches long.

Almost as soon as he is born, the male angler starts looking for a wife. When he finds her, he fastens onto her side with his mouth. Soon their skin grows together. After this they can never be parted. Now he will never lose her in the dark.

The male angler has no fishing rod. He does not need one. His wife does the fishing for him.

The Sharpshooter

Many fish like to eat insects.
One of these is the archer fish.
Other fish have to catch insects
in their mouths. Not the archer.
He can just shoot them down. He
points his head at a bug and spits.

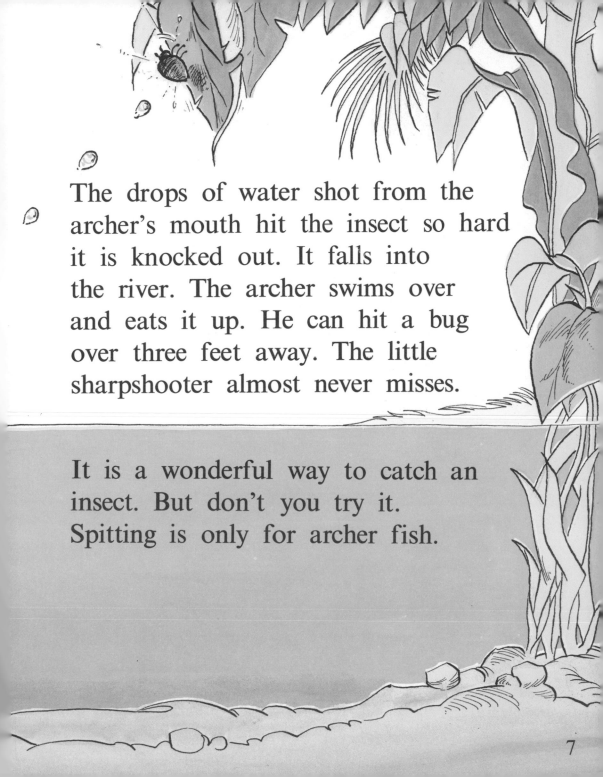

The drops of water shot from the archer's mouth hit the insect so hard it is knocked out. It falls into the river. The archer swims over and eats it up. He can hit a bug over three feet away. The little sharpshooter almost never misses.

It is a wonderful way to catch an insect. But don't you try it. Spitting is only for archer fish.

Look Out For Sharks

All that you may ever see of a shark at sea is his dark fin cutting through the water. If you want to see more, go to an aquarium. It is safer.

Sharks are very mean-looking fish. Some of them are as mean as they look. Some of them will even eat people.

Even a shark's skin is dangerous. It is covered with tiny sharp scales. The scales are like little teeth. Swimmers have been hurt just brushing against a shark.

The great white shark is a huge fish. In his great mouth there are rows and rows of terrible teeth. He is one of the worst man-eaters.

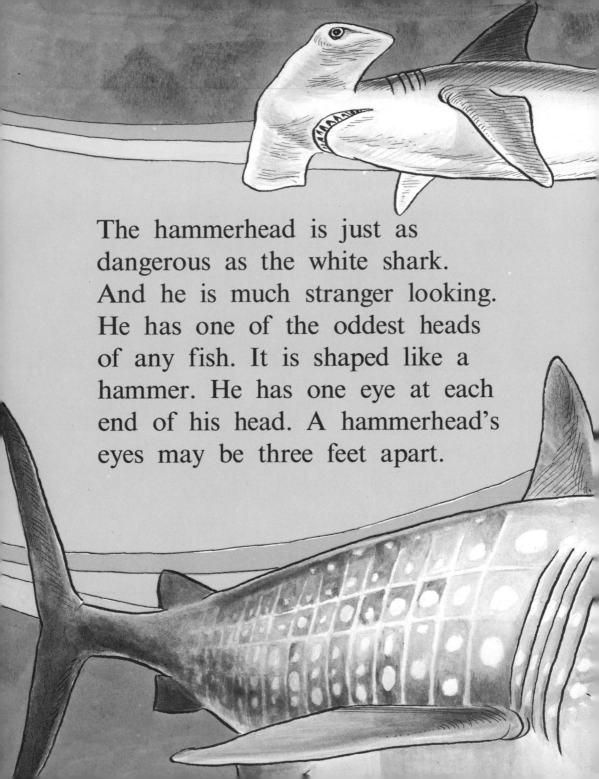

The hammerhead is just as dangerous as the white shark. And he is much stranger looking. He has one of the oddest heads of any fish. It is shaped like a hammer. He has one eye at each end of his head. A hammerhead's eyes may be three feet apart.

The biggest fish in the sea is a shark. He is called the whale shark. But this giant fish eats only tiny fish and plants. He does not eat people. A whale shark may even let people ride on him!

It would not be wise to try to ride any other kind of shark. Other sharks cannot be trusted.

They may attack at any time.
And if there is blood in the
water, it drives them crazy.
If a fish or a person has been
hurt, the sea may suddenly be
full of sharks. They attack
wildly. If one of the sharks
is hurt, the others turn on
him. They do not mind eating
each other.

But most of the time, a shark
will look things over
before he attacks.

A deep-sea diver
may find himself
looking right into the face of
a big shark. If the diver stays
quiet, the shark will probably
go away. Most sharks would
rather eat fish than people.

There is a silly story that a
shark will go away if you
hit him on the nose. Sometimes dolphins will do
this to fight off a
shark. Dolphins are
wonderful swimmers. It is
all right for them to try
it. It is not a good idea
for anyone else.

The Hitchhiker

The remora can travel for thousands of miles beneath the sea without swimming. He has a wonderful way of getting around. He just catches a ride on a bigger fish.

The remora holds on with the top of his head. The top of his head is flat. There is a suction cap on it. With this cap he can quickly fasten onto another fish. He cannot fall off unless he wants to.

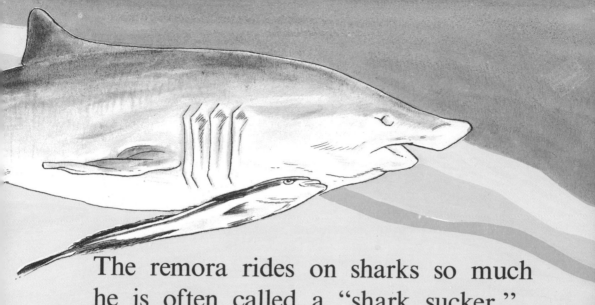

The remora rides on sharks so much
he is often called a "shark sucker."
Sometimes many remoras will ride
on the same shark at the same time.
But remoras will ride on almost any
big fish.

The remora gets a free ride. And he
also gets free meals. When the big
fish catches his dinner, the remora
lets go. He swims around and eats
up the leftovers. And sometimes he
just lets go and goes off fishing for
himself.

Some people use the little remora to
help them catch big fish or turtles.
These fishermen tie a line to the
remora's tail. Then they get in their
boat. They paddle away from shore.
When they see a turtle, they let out
their fishing line. Away goes the
remora.

The remora quickly fastens onto
the turtle. The men in the boat
pull the remora in. The turtle is
caught just as surely as if it had
been hooked. That shows how strong
the remora's suction cap is. He is
one little fish that really uses his
head.

The Sleeping Beauty

Most fish can breathe only under water. If they are out of water too long they die. The African lungfish is not like other fish. He can live out of water for years. He can breathe air.

The lungfish needs to be able to breathe air. In Africa the hot summer sun may dry up the stream where he lives. Before the stream is all dried up, the lungfish curls up in the mud on the bottom. He leaves a tiny hole in the mud to breathe through. He wraps his tail over his eyes.

The mud gets hard and dry. This does not matter to the lungfish. He is asleep. He will sleep until the rains come. The rains will fill the streams again. They will wash him free of his mud ball.

While a lungfish is in his mud ball
he can be dug out of the ground. He
can be sent to an aquarium far from
his home. At the aquarium the mud
ball is opened. This must be done
with great care. If the mud ball
breaks, so will the lungfish.

The lungfish has had nothing
to eat or drink for a long time.
He is much smaller than he
was when he went to sleep. He
is wrinkled and dry and still
curled up.

In a tank of water he straightens out. He eats and eats. Soon he is fatter than ever. He will be all right if he is left alone.

He does not even like another lungfish to share his tank. Sometimes young lungfish will live together for a while without fighting. Then one will bite off the fins and scales of the other. Luckily for lungfish, they can grow new ones. That is one more strange thing about this strange fish from Africa.

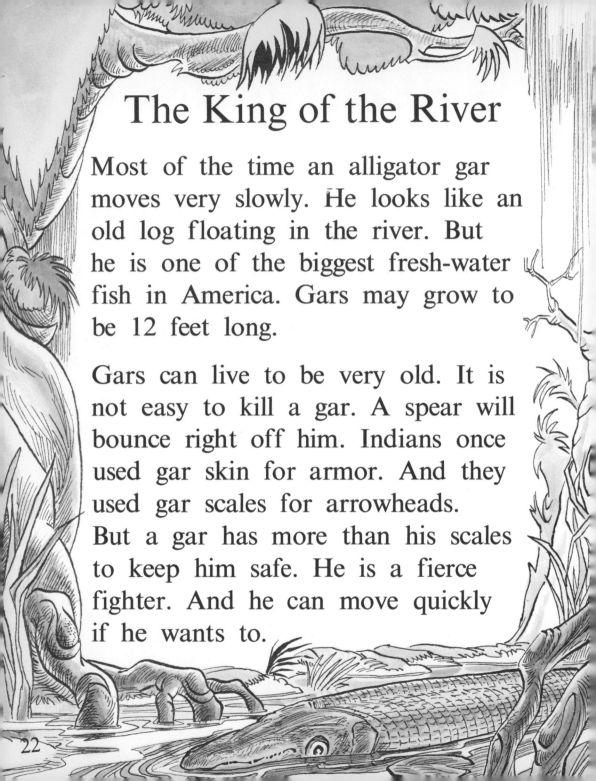

The King of the River

Most of the time an alligator gar moves very slowly. He looks like an old log floating in the river. But he is one of the biggest fresh-water fish in America. Gars may grow to be 12 feet long.

Gars can live to be very old. It is not easy to kill a gar. A spear will bounce right off him. Indians once used gar skin for armor. And they used gar scales for arrowheads. But a gar has more than his scales to keep him safe. He is a fierce fighter. And he can move quickly if he wants to.

The gar may look something like an alligator. But he can kill an alligator with one bite of his mighty jaws.

For millions of years, alligator gars have been the kings of the southern rivers. But they have never been known to attack a person in the water. So don't worry if that old floating log turns out to be a gar.

The Fish With Whiskers

One of the strangest of the river fish is the catfish. Most catfish have eight long feelers on their faces. The feelers make the catfish look as if he has whiskers.

The feelers help a catfish find his food. He can taste with his feelers. He can taste with the rest of his body, too. A catfish can even taste with his tail.

24

The catfish tastes everything he touches. There cannot be many tastes the catfish does not like. Even garbage is fine food for a catfish. This is lucky for us. The catfish helps to keep our rivers clean.

But there is a time when many male catfish do not eat a thing. This is when the eggs are laid by the mother catfish. The father takes the eggs into his mouth. But he does not swallow them.

The father catfish keeps the eggs
in his mouth until they hatch.
Then he just spits the baby catfish out. But he does not leave
the little ones. If he sees an
enemy, he takes the babies right
back into his mouth.

Then one day the father
no longer knows his
children. He would be
glad to eat them himself.
Somehow the young catfish know
this. From then on they will
take care of themselves.

There are more than a thousand kinds of catfish. They are all strange. One of the strangest lives in Africa. He is not at all like the others.

Most catfish stay near the bottom of a river. Not this African catfish. He looks for his food at the top. He rolls over on his back. He swims along upside down. Because of this, he is called the upside-down catfish. Can you think of a better name for him? Even other catfish might find this one strange.

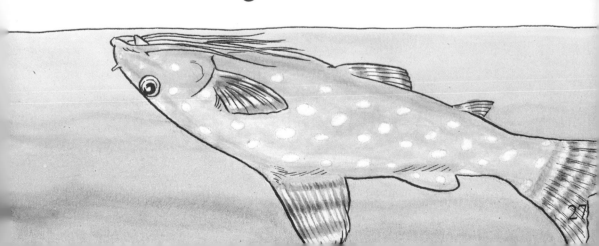

The Great Journey

The beautiful king salmon spends
almost all his life on a journey.
The journey is one of the longest
and strangest in the world of fish.

The journey begins in a little pool
far from the sea. This is where
the salmon are born.

When the baby salmon are a few inches long, they leave their pool. They swim into a stream. The stream grows larger. Other streams join it. The streams become a river. The river now is full of thousands of small salmon. The river is taking them to the sea. It sweeps the salmon over rocks and waterfalls. It sweeps them along tail first! Some of the salmon may have to go two thousand miles to reach the Pacific Ocean. That is a long way to go tail first.

Suddenly the little fish are in the huge ocean. They will live here for about three years. They will swim hundreds and hundreds of miles. They may swim far away from land out into the deep Pacific.

As they swim they eat and eat. They grow bigger and bigger. They grow stronger and stronger. They will need to be strong. The hardest part of their journey is about to begin. Suddenly the salmon stop eating. Somehow they know that it is time to go back to the same little pools they left so long ago.

How can the salmon do this? Salmon have a wonderful sense of smell. They have wonderful memories, too. They remember the smell of the water in the pools where they were born. They now must follow their noses back to their birthplace.

It was easy for the young salmon to come down the rivers to the sea. The rivers just carried them. But now the salmon must go the other way. They must swim against the mighty rivers. They must leap up the waterfalls. They must fight against the waters of the rapids.

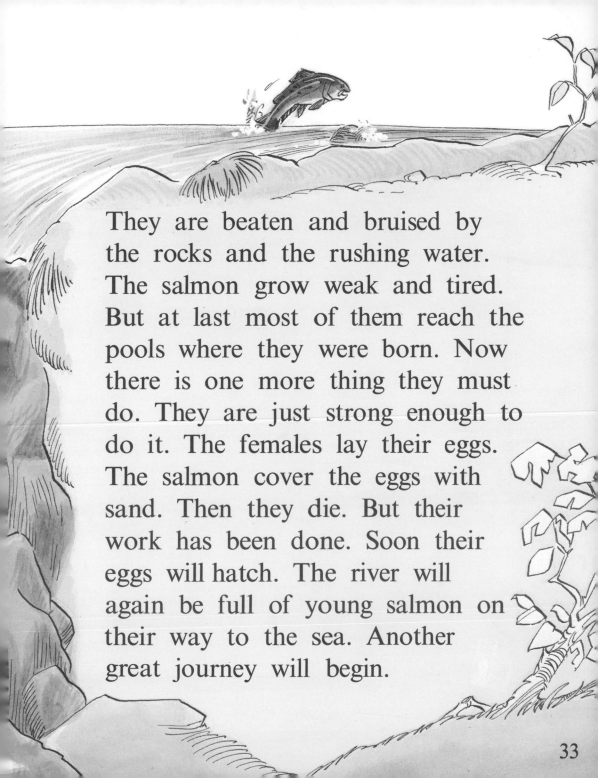

They are beaten and bruised by
the rocks and the rushing water.
The salmon grow weak and tired.
But at last most of them reach the
pools where they were born. Now
there is one more thing they must
do. They are just strong enough to
do it. The females lay their eggs.
The salmon cover the eggs with
sand. Then they die. But their
work has been done. Soon their
eggs will hatch. The river will
again be full of young salmon on
their way to the sea. Another
great journey will begin.

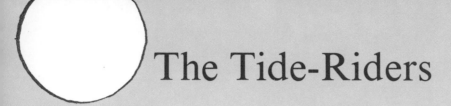

The Tide-Riders

Every day the waters of the oceans rise and fall. When the water is low it is called low tide. When it is high it is called high tide. Every two weeks there is a very high tide. There are little fish who seem to know all about the tides. They are called grunion.

At night in the spring and summer thousands of grunion swim up onto the California beaches. They swim up on the very high tide. The waves go out. The grunion are left on the beach. Right away the female grunion start digging. They dig with their tails.

Soon they are half buried in the soft, wet sand. Then they lay their eggs. They must do this before the next wave comes in. When the next wave comes in the grunion wiggle down to it. It takes them back to the sea.

The eggs stay in the sand for two weeks. Then the next very high tide washes over them. Out pop the baby grunion. The waves carry them out to sea. They will stay in the sea for a year. Then they will ride the tide back to the beaches to lay their own eggs.

The Great Mystery

Eels are strange creatures. They look like snakes. They move like snakes. But they are fish.

For thousands of years eels had a secret. How were young eels born? Where were they born? Nobody knew. Nobody had ever seen an eel egg. Nobody had ever seen a baby eel. The secret of the eels was found out far from their fresh-water homes.

Out in the Atlantic Ocean men had seen fish that looked like tiny glass leaves. Two men caught a few of these fish and kept them in a tank of water. The men had a big surprise. The tiny fish turned into little eels.

Now men knew that eels came from the sea. But how did they get there? A man named Johannes Schmidt wanted to find out. He asked ships' captains to help him. The captains watched for the tiny glass fish. They caught many for Dr. Schmidt. For 17 years he studied them. At last he knew the secret of the eels.

Female eels live most of their lives
far from the sea. They live in ponds
and rivers and streams. Some even
live in wells. Then the time comes
for them to lay their eggs. They
swim down the rivers to the ocean.
There the male eels are waiting for
them. Together they swim out into
the ocean. They swim and swim.
At last they come to a place called
the Sargasso Sea. All the eels from
Europe and America come there. And
there, deep in the sea, they lay
their eggs. Then they die.

After a week the eggs hatch. The baby eels now look like glass leaves. They look just like the ones Dr. Schmidt studied. The baby American eels float and swim toward America. The baby European eels move toward Europe. No one knows how this can be. That is one secret the eels still keep to themselves.

Before they reach the rivers, the little glass fish change into little eels. The females leave the males. The females find homes far from the ocean. Years go by. They grow strong and fat. Then one day they start back down the rivers. They meet the waiting male eels. Together they will make the long, long journey back to the Sargasso Sea.

The Balloon

The puffer fish is small. He is a slow swimmer. But he has a wonderful way of keeping himself safe. When he sees a big fish coming he does not swim away. He just puffs himself up.

He does this by swallowing air or water. This makes him look like a balloon.

The big fish may be scared away by this sudden change. If the big fish is not scared away, he will find that the round puffer is quite a mouthful.

The strangest puffer of all is called the porcupine fish. His skin is covered with sharp scales. When he puffs himself up, his scales stick out all over. Any fish that swallowed him would have a very sore throat.

Sometimes puffers do a silly thing. They keep on puffing up and puffing up until—POP goes the puffer.

Old Big Nose

The swordfish has the longest and sharpest "nose" in the world of fish. It is really part of his jaw. It has two very sharp edges. It is shaped like a big flat sword. And the swordfish uses it like a sword.

Into a school of fish the mighty
swordfish swims. He slashes his
sword all around. Soon he has cut
up a fine meal for himself.

The swordfish likes to eat fish. And many people like to eat swordfish. But swordfish are not easy to catch. Nets cannot hold them. They slash their way out with their swords.

Today men have learned how to catch swordfish with hooks. This is much safer for men than it used to be. Swordfish used to be speared with harpoons. Often the swordfish would fight back. He might even attack the boat. The swordfish is so fast and so strong he can run his sword right into a wooden boat.

Sometimes sailors on the boat were badly hurt. Sometimes the boat would even sink to the bottom of the sea.

The swordfish's sword is a mighty weapon. But he is not born with it. The baby swordfish has teeth. As he grows, so does his sword. He loses his teeth. He does not need teeth with that sword.

The Fish With Wings

The flying fish looks like a little model airplane. But the flying fish does not fly. He glides.

The flying fish swims to the top of the water as fast as he can. He skims along for a bit. Then he flips his tail and up he goes.

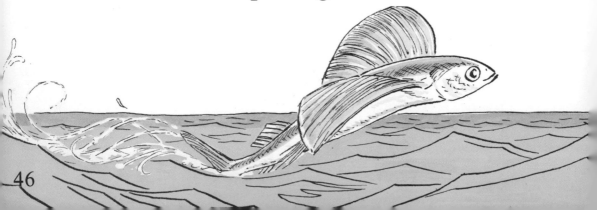

We think the flying fish leaves the water to get away from his enemies. He can stay in the air for almost a minute. Then down he comes with a splash. Often he will just flip his tail and take off again.

The winds may carry him high above the water. Sometimes at night flying fish will glide right onto the deck of a boat. They may have gotten away from a hungry dolphin. But now they will be a wonderful breakfast for a hungry sailor.

The Flying Saucers

Rays are strange-looking fish. Some of them are very small. Some of them are very big. Most of them are very, very flat.

The round sting ray is a small ray. He is as round and flat as a plate. He lives along the seashore. He likes muddy water. He is the color of mud. It is hard to see him lying flat in the mud.

It is not hard for the sting ray to see you. His eyes are on top of his head. This helps him to watch out for enemies.

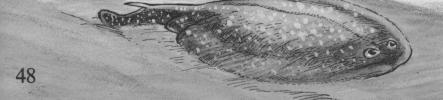

The sting ray has a strange way of fighting his enemies. He fights with his tail. On his tail he has a stinger. There is poison on the stinger. It is a terrible weapon.

People may step on round sting rays by mistake. People who do can be badly hurt. If you think there are sting rays around, drag your feet. The rays will get out of your way. Like everyone else, the sting ray does not like to be stepped on.

The little round sting ray does not
go out into the deep sea. But there
are many rays that do. The sea is
the home of the biggest ray of all.
He is the manta ray. He is called
"the giant devil fish." That sounds
fierce. But he is not. He has no
stinger. And he eats only very
small fish. He sweeps them into
his mouth as he swims.

It is wonderful to watch a
manta swimming. His sides
flap up and down like huge
wings. He looks like a big
black bat flying under water.

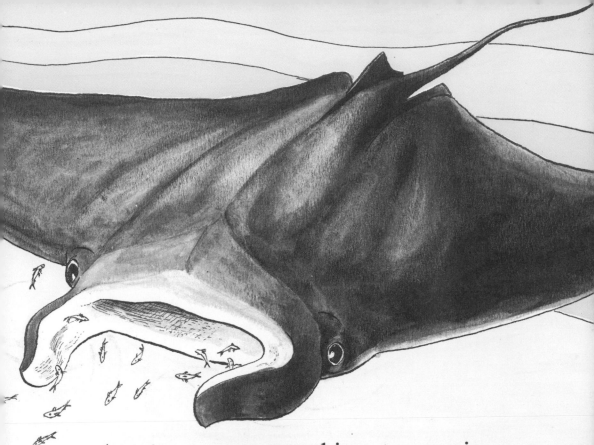

An even stranger thing to see is
a manta leaping. He jumps high
in the air. When the giant manta
comes down, he comes down with
a giant crash. Sometimes two or
three mantas will all leap at once.
The great crash of their landing
sounds like thunder across the sea.

The Hanger-On

In the sea there is a tiny
fish that does not look at
all like a fish. He is called
the sea horse. When you
see him you know why. His
head is like the head of a
tiny, tiny horse. But the
rest of him is not shaped
like a horse. It is not
shaped like a fish, either.
It is just strange.

One very strange thing about
the sea horse is his tail. He
can hang onto things with it
the way a monkey can.

Most of the time the sea horse just hangs onto plants under water. When he wants to go to another plant, he lets go. He swims away.

He does not swim the way other fish do. It looks as if he is standing on his tail. And he swims very slowly.

There is only one part of the sea horse that moves fast. It is the tiny fin on his back. Back and forth it goes. It pushes the sea horse through the water to another plant.

It is lucky that the slow sea horse does not have to chase his food. He just sucks in bits of food that float by. He has no teeth.

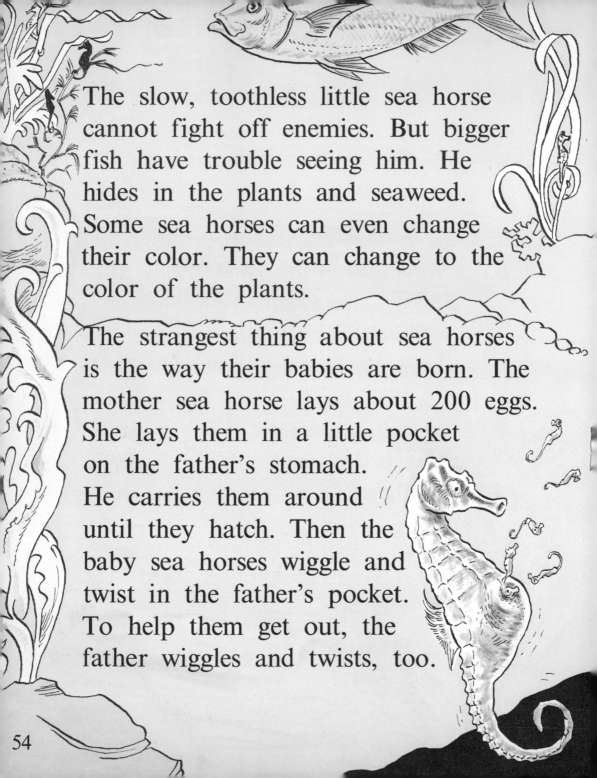

The slow, toothless little sea horse cannot fight off enemies. But bigger fish have trouble seeing him. He hides in the plants and seaweed. Some sea horses can even change their color. They can change to the color of the plants.

The strangest thing about sea horses is the way their babies are born. The mother sea horse lays about 200 eggs. She lays them in a little pocket on the father's stomach. He carries them around until they hatch. Then the baby sea horses wiggle and twist in the father's pocket. To help them get out, the father wiggles and twists, too.

The babies pop out into the sea.
Right away the baby sea horses
start grabbing at things with their
tails. They have not learned what
to hold onto. They may even try to
hold onto air bubbles. They soon
learn. They find a plant. They hang
onto it and watch the underwater
world go by.

The Tree-Climber

You never know where you may find a fish. But what a surprise it would be to find a fish in a tree. It happens. There really is a fish that can climb a tree! His name is the mud-skipper.

The mud-skipper climbs trees to catch insects. He pulls himself up the tree with his front fins. They are almost like little legs. He cannot climb very high. But it is amazing that a fish can climb a tree at all.

The mud-skipper spends some time in the water. But he is out of the water as much as he is in it.

He walks and skips and jumps around on the mud flats. When he wants to skip quickly, he pushes himself along with his tail. He can skip faster than a man can follow him. It is a funny sight to see a mud-skipper skip.

The mud-skipper does so many things that are strange for a fish to do. Do you suppose the mud-skipper knows that he is a fish?

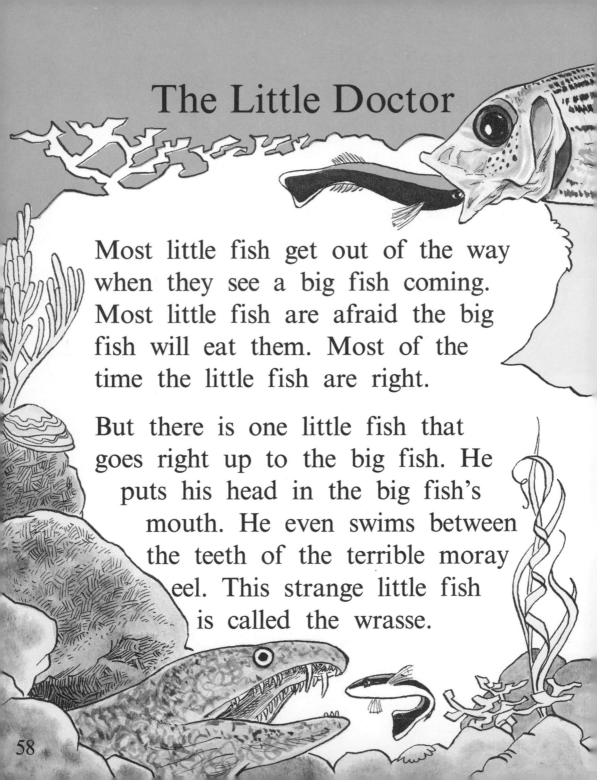

The Little Doctor

Most little fish get out of the way when they see a big fish coming. Most little fish are afraid the big fish will eat them. Most of the time the little fish are right.

But there is one little fish that goes right up to the big fish. He puts his head in the big fish's mouth. He even swims between the teeth of the terrible moray eel. This strange little fish is called the wrasse.

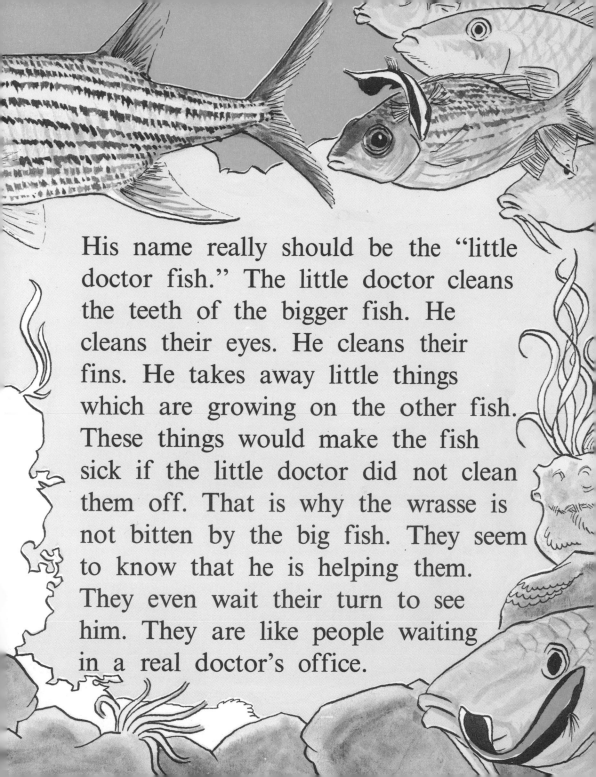

His name really should be the "little doctor fish." The little doctor cleans the teeth of the bigger fish. He cleans their eyes. He cleans their fins. He takes away little things which are growing on the other fish. These things would make the fish sick if the little doctor did not clean them off. That is why the wrasse is not bitten by the big fish. They seem to know that he is helping them. They even wait their turn to see him. They are like people waiting in a real doctor's office.

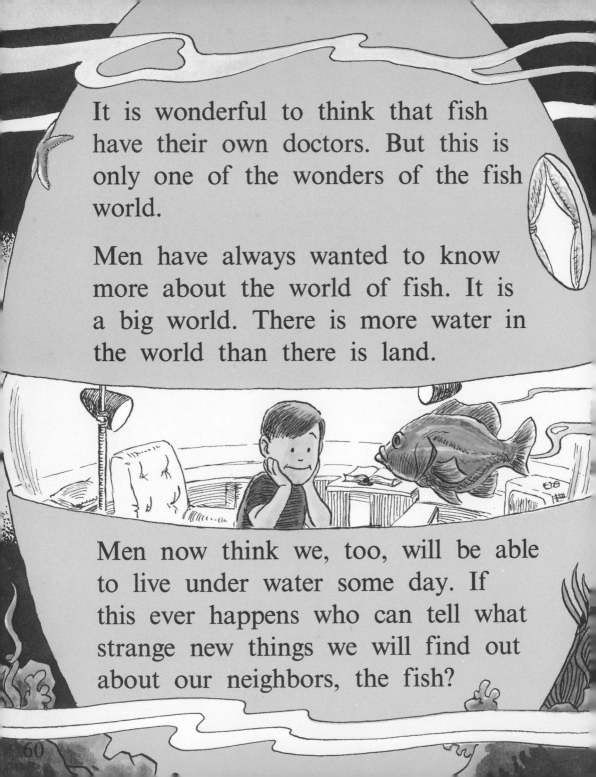

It is wonderful to think that fish have their own doctors. But this is only one of the wonders of the fish world.

Men have always wanted to know more about the world of fish. It is a big world. There is more water in the world than there is land.

Men now think we, too, will be able to live under water some day. If this ever happens who can tell what strange new things we will find out about our neighbors, the fish?

The
STEP-UP Books

NATURE LIBRARY

ANIMALS DO THE STRANGEST THINGS

BIRDS DO THE STRANGEST THINGS

FISH DO THE STRANGEST THINGS

INSECTS DO THE STRANGEST THINGS

Story of AMERICA

Meet THE NORTH AMERICAN INDIANS

Meet THE MEN WHO SAILED THE SEAS

Meet CHRISTOPHER COLUMBUS

Meet THE PILGRIM FATHERS

Meet BENJAMIN FRANKLIN

Meet GEORGE WASHINGTON

Meet THOMAS JEFFERSON

THE ADVENTURES OF LEWIS AND CLARK

Meet ANDREW JACKSON

Meet ABRAHAM LINCOLN

Meet ROBERT E. LEE

Meet THEODORE ROOSEVELT

Meet JOHN F. KENNEDY

Meet MARTIN LUTHER KING, JR.

THE STORY OF FLIGHT